Beneath the Palms

A Poetry Collection

Danielle Klahr

BookLeaf Publishing

India | USA | UK

Copyright © Danielle Klahr
All Rights Reserved.

This book has been self-published with all reasonable efforts taken to make the material error-free by the author. No part of this book shall be used, reproduced in any manner whatsoever without written permission from the author, except in the case of brief quotations embodied in critical articles and reviews.

The Author of this book is solely responsible and liable for its content including but not limited to the views, representations, descriptions, statements, information, opinions, and references ["Content"]. The Content of this book shall not constitute or be construed or deemed to reflect the opinion or expression of the Publisher or Editor. Neither the Publisher nor Editor endorse or approve the Content of this book or guarantee the reliability, accuracy, or completeness of the Content published herein and do not make any representations or warranties of any kind, express or implied, including but not limited to the implied warranties of merchantability, fitness for a particular purpose.

The Publisher and Editor shall not be liable whatsoever...

Made with ❤ on the BookLeaf Publishing Platform

www.bookleafpub.in
www.bookleafpub.com

For Maia,

my favorite poet.

Acknowledgement

First and foremost, I'd like to thank my family for their unwavering support. Rudy, Paul, and Maia, the three of you mean more to me than I could ever say. I'm so grateful for our little family. After a particularly difficult year I'm reminded of how we lean on each other and get through life's obstacles as a team. I laugh hardest when we're all together. I love you three like crazy.

To my parents and siblings, I miss and love you all so much. Living away from you has been one of the hardest things I've ever done, but it's allowed me to grow and thrive in ways I never imagined. When you read these poems (and I know you will, because you always seem to be proud of me no matter what I do or screw up), I hope you'll recognize the inspiration and impact you've had on me and what I'm moved to write about.

Though nearly two decades have passed, my love of poetry and literature was born during my undergraduate studies at the University at Albany. Studying poets like Sylvia Plath, Gwendolyn Brooks, Langston Hughes, Czesław Miłosz, Adrienne Rich, and so many others lit a fire inside of me that has smoldered, though ever so slightly, ever since. Thank you to the UAlbany English Department for igniting that flame.

I need to also give a shout out to the beautiful nature of Florida, where I've lived for close to four years now. I never tire of the palm trees and sunsets, along with the wildlife that seems so exotic to this girl from the Northeast. You'll notice the scenery has inspired many of the poems in *Beneath the Palms*, and will likely continue to do so in future writings.

And finally, thank you to the readers of this collection. Putting this book together has been thrilling and terrifying all at once. Poetry is so personal, and laying my thoughts and feelings out on display in this way is uncomfortable. But, discomfort leads to growth and I am here for it! I hope you are too.

Preface

This project began on a whim. I hadn't written or studied poetry for nearly twenty years, and I was both surprised and delighted by how naturally it returned to me. What I love most about poetry is the absence of rules in both writing and reading. Poems do not need to rhyme or conform to specific formats. A poem is art comprised of language, meaning derived from the context of words as well as their appearance on the page. Each line break, each stanza, each punctuation mark and capital or lowercase letter is deliberate. All of these components woven together creates a unique experience for the reader, independent of the poet's meaning, intention, or inspiration. Be mindful of this as you read *Beneath the Palms*.

Danielle Klahr
February 2025

Away in a moment

It fades,
the ripple on smooth water
disturbed for a moment,
gradually calming and
absorbed into the black lake
the cause gone
before it could be named,
washed away in a moment.

Focused on the surface,
now a mirror to the sun
which begins to dip lower
lower until it touches earth,
billowing deep hues of
orange and magenta
across the sky.

Spreading over the water
a blanket of fire
searing the surface,
ever-changing in the moment.

It also fades,
burning flames become
cooling embers reflecting
from the sky and eventual
darkness to nothing.

The morning waters
like a window after
a bath too hot.
Billowy clouds of mist
hover over stretched silk
menacing in its silence.

The fog, too, fades
dissolved into icy tendrils
until it is gone.
Left is the glassy calm,
ever-present despite
any disturbance.

An errant ripple from
tossed rock,
reflections of sky
blue or ablaze,
dense cotton clouds
hung low.
Often-occurring distractions
distinct from alteration.

Beneath the Palms

On the day of my birth, 48 years later,
I sit beneath the palms beside a shimmering
pool reflecting blue skies and warm bright
sunlight. Reflecting, myself, on events that
have led to this moment, all I've learned, and
dreaming of what's to come.

Dreams have shape, some long and drawn
out, some short, some with girth. Too many
fuzzy and hard to decipher while others
solid and sharp, fully formed. Mine shift
shapes, a constant metamorphosis
sometimes clear and often confusing,
pulsing and quivering as they change form.

I have perhaps 30 years more, give or
take. Is that enough time to reign in a
dream? To hone, to focus, to perfect?
To mold, form it into something real
instead of allowing it a life of its own?

Yes.
I believe it is.

River Camp

Smooth rush
over gentle curve
diving into clear and cool.
Subtle spray
repeated infinitely.

Meandering waters
make leisurely way
among emerald pines lush and long.
Muddy banks
carved softly.

Tiny fins
and luminous scales
darting frantically in calm currents.
Smoothed rock
in slimy silt.

Gazing from
lush grass and pebbles
memories preserved in this place.
Longing for those
long gone.

Goddess of Spring

Goddess of Spring
Joy in human form
Sunlight as a girl
Exuding love and rapture

She stands pure and giddy
Feet bare against the grass
Squealing with delight as
She darts across the yard
Streams of chilly water
Follow, chasing, racing

She turns about
Runs again
Directly into the stream
Hopping, bouncing,
Dripping wet, pushing
Drenched hair from her eyes

Again, again! she
Commands with a giggle
Her laugh is my favorite song
I run to her with a squeal of
My own hand in hand as
We dart through the spray

A moment in time
Ordinary and plain
Cherished like her
Small hand in mine

In otherwise
bustling days

Safely secured
affection in abundance
at my request
You smile and spread
your arms outstretched
then folded, encircling
my frame
I sigh softly
face nuzzled into shoulder
nose grazing the softness
of your neck
With deep steady breath
I inhale your skin
a scent so specific
and sweet
Tension melts away
flows and puddles
at my feet now on tiptoe
reaching lips to cheek

Such small, slow moments
in otherwise bustling days
bring life to my heart
and calm to my mind
Unguardedly
loving and loved.

Sunflowers and Lilacs

It occurs to me that we share
favorite hues now, colors
overlooked in my childhood.
Immersed in turquoise,
blues and black
yearning for contrast.

Now I notice myself seeking
them out, my choice for
clothing, accessories, decor,
and favorite flowers
fragrant and alive with
pretty pigments so familiar,
somehow similar, yet distinct.

Purple the color of my birthstone,
born from you.
Yellow the color of sunshine,
my daughter's lullaby.
Love passed on like
a tossed bouquet from a
garden in full bloom,
perennials tended and cared for.

You & I

You are bright, brilliant
perfection.
I am childish and ridiculous
squirming in my skin.

I open my mouth
then instantly question and
admonish myself.
Awkward and squeamish
while you speak eloquently.

You are kind, forgiving
comforting.
I am angry, embarrassing
terrified of myself.

I listen to you
and am amazed by
what you know.
Empathetic and understanding
while I smolder from inside.

You are gentle, caring
loving.
I am loved and cared for
grateful for your pardon.

Lady Palm

Long and lean she waves and sways
simply beautiful
symbolic of vacation mode
now I live below her.
With the breeze she bends
gentle calmness in her rustle
lining paths of shimmering sands
and asphalt just the same.
A grouping here, a row there
or solitary among clouds
always striking
never disappointing
my gaze on cascading fronds
atop a tall, thin, imperfect line.
Her silhouette stunning
against the dropping sun
set off by oranges, pinks, and violets
no longer green
but dark, nearly black
breathtaking just the same.

SO-SO

I would shout when I was young
    so confident, so assured.
Ensuring my voice was heard
    by audiences consenting or opposed.

As I grew I began to shrink
    so small, so insignificant.
Fearing reaction to my words
    my silence a comfort and a shame.

A woman cowering from herself
    so scared, so unsure.
Thoughts became confounding riddles
    to be decoded in solitude.

Yearning to speak up as I had
    so bold, so brave.
Wondering what it will take
    to remove shackles self-imposed.

Wily and wild

Pruned and perfected
Tamed overnight
Only for moments

Shortened and sheared
Blooms in the dark
Apparent by dawn

Growth and glory
Returning to beauty
No longer barren

Looming and large
Nearly unwieldy
Breadth without limits

Wily and wild
Becoming a hindrance
Must be contained

Pruned and perfected
Tamed overnight
Only for moments

Cobalt Space

Everyone does the best they can,
I truly do believe.
Yet any time we disagree
there isn't much reprieve.

Forgiveness starts with understanding
truth is not concrete.
We have ways of viewing things
to make others obsolete.

What is right? What is wrong?
Sometimes it's hard to tell.
I often wonder silently,
my mind inside its shell.

Lost in thought, lost in myself,
cut off and locked away.
Sinking into cobalt space,
and I am not okay.

Connection is what brings me back
no longer lost, but weary.
That one small piece of common ground
an answer to my query.

Soft

Soft
ground with the
sensation of
sinking into
pillowy earth.
Shrieks and
giggles surrounding.
Resounding.
Through the noise
the squeak of
rusty chains
back and forth on
a sturdy metal frame.
Legs stretched
long hair floating
people small
young
not yet changed.
Changed their minds
no longer interested
in games played
in grass sharp and
soft.

An unprepared journey

I take a tentative step.
My feet are cold. Bare.
The sensation is rough, sharp
textures nearly pierce
but I press on.
My steps continue slowly
balanced and precise
moving forward
eyes fixed down
not up, not ahead.

I don't know what to expect
I know what I feel
rough, cold, wet, sharp.
I can't help but wonder if
it will always be this way
hopeful my unprepared journey
will end in comfort.

Longing for softness, for
warm light to bathe my limbs
I run my hands over my arms
smooth skin dry and cool
the sensation in my hand
more pleasing than my soles.
I already hold what I seek.

The Hum

Quietly it starts to buzz
    an insect to my ear.
Slowly it begins to rise
    and I begin to leer.

It makes no difference when I look
    the hum maintains its din.
It builds and multiplies around me
    pleading *let me in.*

Though I resist the sound as best I can
    the noise is overpowering.
I am no match, the fight is gone
    my body shivers, cowering.

Steady, deeply I take a breath
    willing my nerves to calm.
Aware I have a choice to make
    blooming bud or bomb.

In her own way

There within reach,
but a stretch
she doesn't notice, wanting,
yearning, wishing,
thinking of something that
is not yet.
Yet, in her own way
possessed but unseen
deep within
as if swallowed.
She gulps
gently pushes in her own way
out of her way
thoughts, feelings, fear moved
altered but apparent
In her way no longer.
Her own.

Vital Sacrifice

Green leaves with a crunch
piled with colors vivid and crisp
and lean flavorless meats
all carefully tallied.

Feet land with a crunch
on autumn leaves, faster, faster
burning without fire or smoke
strained then stretched with purpose.

Muscles squeeze with a crunch
focused on form and breath
feet planted, chin tilted
intentional pain and release.

Ice fractures with a crunch
penetrating glacial waters
sinking lower, deeper
until time is up.

Joints grind with a crunch
bones jutting, writhing beneath
pale skin, translucent gray.
Vitality gives way to pursuit.

In the shadows

Stumbling, slurring
bewildered
a struggle to
recall what happened
barely a whisper
just out of reach
are memories there
but not quite
in the shadows
illuminated
by the knowing
without remembering
the spoken words
or viscous actions
from times before.

Rebirth

Stepping into dawn
enveloped by wet heavy air
heated already by awakened sun.

Inhaling deeply the familiar scent
plentiful here but fleeting
where I come from.

The fragrance of fertile earth
ripe with life and
impending growth.

Earthy pleasant perfume
wafts of warmth rise
and swirl around me.

The aroma reminiscent of
spring afternoons
following a frigid winter.

Here, each morning is spring
a damp and dirty rebirth
savored in blossoming sunlight.

Showtime

Please refrain
Relax, relax
Just sit back and enjoy
This rehearsed display
of love, of loss,
of sorrow, and of joy.

Take in the colors
Feel the notes
Each scene its own display
Immerse yourself
In this staged world
Leading your mind astray.

Forget the future
Forget the past
Live in the here and now
Open yourself
To learning, feeling
and you'll be changed somehow.

Raptor

To my amusement
the raptor looms
in silent circles
wings outstretched like
the arms of a mother
inviting her child into
a loving embrace.
Its only movement
a graceful glide
around, spirals against
darkened skies heavy
with smoky clouds
thick like foam.
Menacing swirls
surveying from above
for vulnerable prey while
earthly creatures move
unknowingly through their
redundant days.

Love, Mom

Each day I wait to hear your stories
what you learned, who you talked to,
how you felt and why.
Feeling proud of your independence
while missing times when I was your world.
Knowing every friend, every classmate,
talking to your teachers and
aware of every detail.
That wouldn't be appropriate
now that you're grown
but what I wouldn't give to peek in on you
laughing with your friends at lunch
raising your hand to answer questions in class.
Not to be nosy or overstep, not to pry
just to know you better. More.
When you were a baby, a small child
I couldn't get enough of you.
Your giggle, the sweet smell of your hair
your soft breathing as you slept
the way you would dance and entertain.
Children grow and change so quickly
while adults stay the same, more or less.

It's a cruel fact of motherhood
seldom discussed
but I wouldn't change it, trade it,
or ever let it go
for I was once your whole world, but
you will always be my entire universe.

At first light

I crave the quiet of morning
A glint of newborn light
The tenderness of daybreak
so different from the night

I yearn for the stillness of dawn
The gentle awakening of day
A crisp perfume of earth and dew
Before it floats away

I long for silence at first light
The hush while colors bloom
Opening, unfurling rays
As sun lifts from its tomb

I ache for peaceful early hours
The pause as time unfolds
Ripe with possibilities
And stories not yet told

For Mattie

I listened as you cried and wailed
howling in the dark as you paced
around in circles, refusing to be still.

I held you as you ate your favorite
treat, slowly lapping drops of water
from the shallow bowl in my hands.

I soothed you as best I could
fighting to stay calm, be strong
as we raced toward your relief.

I watched as you slipped away
first into slumber, then gone
in cruel, cherished moments.

I wept once you had passed from us
glad the kids were there, wishing they weren't
holding each other tightly for comfort.

I sobbed when you came back to us
ashes in a carved wooden box
image and imprint placed prominently.

I smile each time I think of you
intelligent, playful, and stubborn
friendly and loved by family and strangers.

We laugh when we tell your stories
your personality unmatched, so loved when
you were here, loved still while you are gone.

Maturity

Youth traded for wisdom
beauty wrung out like a wet rag
droplets clinging to fibers
desperate to endure.

Understanding without judgement
regret chiseled away from memory
carefully carved like soap
curled shavings fall away
revealing soft sculpture
fresh and fragrant.

A lovely form of my own design.

Onward

Moved by a story,
a true one, nonetheless,
of lifelong dreams and
passion across decades.

Body and resolve strengthen
with age, where others wither.
Unwavering pursuit through
creatures and currents.

Undeterred by anguish
and heartache, working
against waves of sea
water and pain.

Fueled by arrested
attempts to finally
achieve what had
never been done.

As I sit comfortably,
pen and paper in hand,
I'm unable to fathom what
what was endured to accomplish
accomplish such a feat.

Obstacles litter the path
to every destination,
yet against this tale
mine seem so small,
nearly insignificant.

If *that* can be done,
surely *this* can be done.
Inspiration propels me
forward, onward, like a
swimmer in the sea.

Night Bandit

Hiding in the crevices
    pressed against the wall
The bandit sits in wait for dark
    so he can steal it all

Comfortable and cozy
    sleeping through the light
An odd appearance in the day
    for he prefers the night

At dusk he starts to stalk
    his prey refuse and putrid trash
You'll barely know if he's been there
    unless you hear a crash

He's fairly harmless unless surprised
    or if you step too near
Sometimes he'll hiss or even growl
    but only out of fear.

Birthday Treats

Squeezing tightly
stinging tears
his sticky hand in mine
enter a room ripe with
crayons and perspiration
the perfume of youth.
Wide blue eyes and
a beaming smile
awe and excitement
mixed with pride
favorite sweets carefully
arranged and shared.
Birthday treats for
a special boy
one small act of
love so meaningful
to a precious child.

In the absence of winter

In the absence of winter
emerald plumage grows while
the heat of light from above
warms earth and air.

Endless life where
color never dies
white apparent only
in billowy clouds hung
against sapphire,
bleached birds picking
through fertile lawns
sloping grasses spilling into
waters glassy and still.

Storms form as gray
covers pastel skies
hurling heavy rains to
feed and quench,
waters sustaining lively hues.

Fast furor swiftly fades
in contrast to unending
spiels of blizzard and squall.
Sweat and steam released
from pavement, vapors
opposed to sleet and slush.

Hushed and calm, still air
cools to comfort
chilling into evening
through night until
the crawl of sunrise,
cozy rays alight with
brilliant heat free
to provide warmth,
unobscured by the
presence of winter.

Scripted beauty

My mother's handwriting,
a series of loops and
steady strokes,
a stark contrast to
my own.

At times I tried to
emulate her cursive,
mostly in school when
permission or excuses
were required.

I couldn't quite capture
the effect, but
it was a close enough
facsimile, never questioned.
No one, save for a friend or two
knew what I had done.

Perhaps my hands are
too shaky,
or my mind in a rush.

It may be that I don't take
the time, or care
to create those perfect lines.

When I write by hand,
nothing more than ink
scratched hastily across paper,
penmanship isn't a thought.
I work to weave words into meaning,
scripted beauty unmatched
by careful loops and lines.

My mother's handwriting,
born of gentle hands,
cannot be perfectly copied
by myself or anyone else.
Daughters, in their youth,
often imitate their mothers
until they can flourish on their own.

What is a Poet?

What is a poet?
Certainly not me
with barely an ounce
of real creativity.
Scribbling, determined
to make an impact
questioning its validity
wondering what it lacked.
Artsy, brilliant, bold
describe a poet's mind
creating images with words
elusive, hard to find.

With shaky hand
I start my script
a beginning with no end.
Who will read it? Who will care?
Should I show family and friends?
Nervous and unsure
I continue down the page
pushing away unnerving thoughts
releasing from the cage
the fear that I'm not good enough

not smart enough or brave
jotting as the words flow out
like cool air from a cave.

Am I a poet?
Perhaps I am or
possibly could be.
What I know is
as I write
I've never been so free.

www.ingramcontent.com/pod-product-compliance
Lightning Source LLC
La Vergne TN
LVHW021252200726
843509LV00012B/1646